THE REMINISCENCES OF
Captain Ralph S. Barnaby
U.S. Navy (Retired)

INTERVIEWED BY
Dr. John T. Mason, Jr.

U.S. Naval Institute • Annapolis, Maryland

Copyright © 1995

Preface

When Dr. John Mason inaugurated the Naval Institute's oral history program in 1969, one of the first retired officers whom he interviewed was Captain Ralph Barnaby. Dr. Mason had the interview tape transcribed and later corrected by Captain Barnaby. Until now, though, it was not indexed nor put into a bound volume, perhaps because the oral history was only a single interview about gliders rather than a full-length oral autobiography. Captain Barnaby had a pioneering career in the areas of soaring and gliding, going back to the time of the Wright brothers. In this interview, he provides glimpses of some ground-breaking steps in the history of naval aviation.

In addition to annotating the transcript, I have done some slight editing in the interest of clarity and smoothness. However, the transcript is still quite close to the original spoken version. Ms. Ann Hassinger of the Naval Institute's history division has made a valuable contribution through her diligence in the overall process of printing, proofreading, and overseeing the binding of the completed volume.

Paul Stillwell
Director, History Division
U.S. Naval Institute
November 1995

CAPTAIN RALPH STANTON BARNABY
U.S. NAVY (RETIRED)

Ralph Stanton Barnaby was recognized as a leading authority on gliders, holder of the National Aeronautical Association Number One Soaring Certificate, a founder-member and fellow of the Institute of Aeronautical Sciences, member of the American Society of Mechanical Engineers, charter member, director, and president of the Soaring Society of America, and author of many technical papers on aeronautical engineering subjects, including a book, Gliders and Gliding (1930). He also managed to combine the unusual qualities of engineering, glider piloting and designing, and sculpture with a naval career.

Born in Meadville, Pennsylvania, on 21 January 1893, he was the son of Charles Weaver Barnaby and Jenny Christy Barnaby. He attended private school in New York City before entering Columbia University, New York, New York, where he was graduated and received the degree of bachelor of mechanical engineering in 1915. In 1945 Columbia awarded him its Medal of Excellence and cited "his many achievements in aeronautics including his experiences in gliding and soaring." The award was in lieu of a degree of master of science or master of arts.

His interest in aviation began in 1908 with the newspaper accounts of Orville Wright's flights at Fort Myer, Virginia, for the Army. During the next three years, Barnaby was busy with model airplane experimentation. In 1909 he designed, built, and flew his first man-carrying glider, and in 1910 founded the New York Model Aero Club. He qualified for membership in the Early Birds, serving as president of that organization, 1941-42. He was assistant chief engineer and head of the engineering department of Standard Aeronautical Corporation, Plainfield, New Jersey, until he enlisted in the United States Navy in December 1917. He was discharged to be commissioned ensign in the U.S. Naval Reserve Force, to date from 26 March 1918. The next year he was commissioned lieutenant (junior grade), Construction Corps, U.S. Navy. Transferred from the Construction Corps to the line of the Navy in 1940, he was designated for aeronautical engineering duty only. He attained the rank of captain on 11 November 1942.

After training at the Naval Aeronautical Ground School, Massachusetts Institute of Technology, Cambridge, Massachusetts, Curtiss Aero and Motor Corporation, and in the Inspectors School, Buffalo, New York, he became assistant inspector, later inspector of naval aircraft in the plant of the L.W.F. Engineering Corporation, College Point, New York. In August 1918 he was ordered overseas to assist with the study of aviation material and European aircraft developments in England and France. Returning to the United States in February 1919, he assisted in the preparation of the NC flying boats for the transatlantic flights of that year.

After three years at the Naval Aircraft Factory, Philadelphia, in November 1922 he reported to the Bureau of Aeronautics as head of the Specifications Section, where he served a total of nine years. He had detached duty for one year, 1928-29, at Wright Field, Dayton, Ohio, as assistant general inspector and material liaison officer with the Engineering Division of the Army Air Corps. In 1929 he was a member of the Klemperer Expedition to investigate soaring conditions in mountainous regions. One of the most important works handled during his duties in the Bureau of Aeronautics was the establishment of the Army-Navy Aircraft Standards Board, through which materials and equipment were brought into uniformity, a great boon to the aircraft industry in general.

In January 1930 he achieved international recognition by making a glider flight from the rigid airship Los Angeles (ZR-3), the first in history. Thereafter, he took part in the first National Soaring Contest at Elmira, New York, and the two succeeding meets in the summers of 1931 and 1932. He was made a member of the National Contest Committee of the National Aeronautics Association. While associated with Rear Admiral William A. Moffett, Chief of the Bureau of Aeronautics, he fashioned a sculptured bust of the admiral, completing it just a few days before the admiral died in the crash of the USS Akron (ZRS-4) in April 1933. That bust and one that Barnaby sculpted of Admiral William S. Sims were placed in Memorial Hall, Bancroft Hall at the Naval Academy.

After 1933 Barnaby served as inspector of naval aircraft, Baltimore, Maryland, and the following year was on duty at the Naval Air Station, Pensacola, Florida, where he sponsored a glider training experiment. He was commended by Secretary of the Navy Claude Swanson in 1935, the letter stating in part as follows:

"Recently there has been brought to my attention your outstanding achievements in the field of gliding and soaring during the last twenty-six years, and more particularly your accomplishments along this line during the last five years. Specifically, on 31 January 1930 you made the first glider descent from an airship, the USS LOS ANGELES. This in itself . . . is worthy of special note. Furthermore, your unusual interest . . . is shown by the continuing record of accomplishment. It is noted that you hold the Number One Soaring license in the United States; that you advocated the use of gliders in preliminary aviation training; that you have taken part in all national soaring meets since 1930. It is further noted that this training and experience, which has been of inestimable benefit to the Navy, has been acquired by you largely on your own initiative and your own time, and at your own expense . . . "

While at the Pensacola Naval Air Station, he was a student of heavier-than-air aviation and was designated a naval aviator on 12 May 1937. The following summer he was ordered to the Fleet Air Base, Coco Solo, Canal Zone. After two years there, he was ordered to the Naval Aircraft Factory, Philadelphia, where he served as chief engineer. The last year of World War II he was commanding officer of the Naval Aircraft Modification Unit, Johnsville, Pennsylvania. He was awarded the Air Medal and Legion of Merit for this period of service.

The Air Medal citation stating in part: " . . . but also personally conducted numerous flight tests of experimental and hazardous nature to prove the feasibility of the techniques he advocated . . ."

Legion of Merit: "For outstanding conduct . . . as Commanding Officer of the Naval Aircraft Modification Unit . . . from June, 1944 to August, 1945. Displaying exceptional foresight, judgment, and professional ability, Captain Barnaby rendered invaluable service in the production of aeronautical equipment and special weapons for immediate use by the combat forces, and by his fine technical skill and tireless efforts, contributed materially to the success of our forces . . . "

Captain Barnaby continued in the latter assignment until relieved of active duty pending his transfer to the retired list of the Navy on 1 January 1947. He later had active duty to represent the Navy at the annual National Soaring Contest, Elmira, New York. In the summer of 1950 he also attended the First World Championship Soaring Competition in Orebro, Sweden, in which 11 nations competed.

Upon his retirement Captain Barnaby became associated with Franklin Institute, Philadelphia, where he was head of the aeronautical activities in laboratories for research and development. Barnaby was married in 1936 to the former Margaret Evans Elston of Columbus, Ohio. She died on 24 February 1981. Captain Barnaby himself died 14 May 1986.

DECLARATION OF TRUST

The undersigned does hereby appoint and designate as his (her) Trustee herein, the Secretary-Treasurer and Publisher of the United States Naval Institute to perform and discharge the following duties, powers, and privileges in connection with the possession and use of a certain taped interview between the undersigned and the Oral History Department of the United States Naval Institute.

(1) As an <u>Open</u> transcript. It may be read (or the tape audited) by qualified researchers upon presentation of proper credentials as determined by the Trustee.

(2) It is expressly understood that in giving this authorization, I am in no way precluded from placing such restrictions as I may desire upon use of the interview at any time during my lifetime, nor does this authorization in any way affect my rights to the copyright of any literary expressions that may be contained in the interview.

Witness my hand and seal this __25th__ day of __November__ 19__69__

Ralph S. Barnaby

I hereby accept and consent to the foregoing Declaration of Trust and the powers therein conferred upon me as Trustee:

R. E. Bowler Jr.
Secretary-Treasurer and Publisher

Interview with Captain Ralph S. Barnaby, U.S. Navy (Retired)
Place: Captain Barnaby's home in Boothbay Harbor, Maine
Date: Wednesday, 27 August 1969
Interviewer: John T. Mason, Jr.

Q: Captain, it's a delight to meet you. I've been really looking forward to this, and to hear from you some of the thrilling, exciting stories about naval aviation, and especially in its early stages. Would you begin by telling me how you, as a rather young man, got interested in aviation?

Captain Barnaby: Well, it really started quite early. I was in school in New York City in 1908, and during that summer I was working as office boy for my father, who was a consulting engineer and had offices in downtown New York. Having a fair amount of spare time on my hands, I read the newspapers. Along in the summer of 1908 I began reading about, first of all, Wilbur Wright's startling flights over in France, and then, of course, Orville Wright's tests before the Army at Fort Myer, Virginia, which resulted in the crash in which Lieutenant Tom Selfridge of the Army was killed.* That got me enthused about aviation. I had thought about it, and I'd done a little kite-flying, but reading of the stories of the Wright brothers actually changed the course of my life, because I was set on an art career.† I dropped back a year in order to get more math in high school and took an engineering course instead, because I wanted to go into aviation.

---

* On 17 September 1908, Lieutenant Thomas Selfridge, USA, rode as a passenger in a plane flown by Orville Wright. During the planned test flight to Alexandria, Virginia, the propeller cut a tail brace wire, and the plane crashed. Selfridge was the first person to be killed in an airplane.
† Barnaby, in fact, became an accomplished sculptor. He later sculpted busts of Admiral William S. Sims and Rear Admiral William A. Moffett for display at Bancroft Hall at the Naval Academy.

Q: Was this typical, sir, of some of your contemporaries also?

Captain Barnaby: I don't know. I imagine a lot of them were inspired by the exploits of the Wrights. I can't tell you. I don't know. I do know that from 1908 on, and even before that, I had thought of a career of flying some way. Of course, I'd never seen anything except some of the old hot-air balloon ascensions and parachutes at country fairs out in Meadville, Pennsylvania, where I was born.

Q: How did your family react to this new interest of yours?

Captain Barnaby: My father was a mechanical engineer, and I don't think he thought that aviation was anything really that you'd go into.

Q: It wasn't a very stable kind of career to go after.

Captain Barnaby: No. As a matter of fact, I still am not sure whether he was wrong or not. But he raised no opposition. He was very pleased to see me go into mechanical engineering, although he would have liked to steer me towards architectural engineering, so I could combine art and engineering.

Q: Yes. It was a very far cry from your original intention of a career in art.

Captain Barnaby Yes, but that's when it started, and in 1909 I designed, built, and flew my first glider, which was before I had ever seen any other heavier-than-air craft fly.

Q: Tell me about that project and how you went about it.

Captain Barnaby: Well, I had built flying models, mostly gliders, because it wasn't until along in 1909 that the rubber-band-powered idea for driving model airplanes became generally known. Of course, that goes clear back, I think, to Pineau in France. His was the rubber-band idea. But most of my models were gliders. I had, of course, read about Lilienthal's experiments, and actually my first glider was patterned more on Lilienthal's gliders than, for instance, on the Wright gliders.* Because I don't think it was until somewhat later that the whole story of the Wright brothers and the wonderful soaring and gliding work they did down at Kitty Hawk got the publicity that it rated.

Q: Did you do this entirely on your own as a solo project, or were you in consultation with somebody who knew something about gliders?

Captain Barnaby: Oh, there was no one who knew any more about it than I did at the time. I did consult my father somewhat on structural design problems, and he would advise me on how to put things together.

Q: Did he get enthusiastic about this too?

Captain Barnaby: Not particularly. I think his only enthusiasm was to see that I didn't build something I was going to break my neck in--to see that it was at least strong enough to do what it was supposed to do. But I don't think he took it seriously at all for a long time.

Q: Where did you try it out?

Captain Barnaby: Well, at that time, in 1909, my father was superintendent of a quartz-grinding mill at Roxbury Falls, Connecticut, which is up the Shepaug River, up toward Litchfield. I went up and spent the summer there. The rest of the family was living in New York City. My father boarded on a farm near the mill, and I went up and spent the summer with him up there. That was where I built this huge glider on this farm.

Q: Was there a bluff or something?

---

* Otto Lilienthal began gliding flights in Germany in 1893. Prior to his death in 1896, he made dozens of flights, including glides of more than 1,000 feet.

Captain Barnaby: There was a large pasture with sufficient slope and sufficient length so that I could make glides down the hillside.

Q: And strong enough air currents?

Captain Barnaby: Not particularly. I didn't do any soaring there. They were just coasting downhill flights which I could do in still air, although the more wind you had, the less your ground speed and the safer it was in that respect. But it was sufficient for me to get short glides. I don't think I ever made any longer than, perhaps 300 feet, getting maybe 10 or 15 feet in the air at the highest part.

Q: Did it all work out happily, or did you have any problems?

Captain Barnaby: Well, it's interesting how closely I followed the Wrights, because my season terminated the same way theirs did with their first powered flight in 1903. I'd finished my gliding and was sitting there thinking it over and talking with my father about it. Then a gust of wind came along and picked the glider up. Before we could rescue it, it had rolled it up in a ball. You know, that's the way the Wrights' experiment ended in 1903 and it ended the 800-and-some-foot flight.* There had been a little damage, I believe, in landing, and they were talking or deciding what to do when the wind picked the thing up and rolled it over on its back and broke it so badly that they decided to call it off for the season. And that's the way my first season of glider flying terminated.

Q: Well, that must have been a very discouraging thing for you.

---

* On 17 December 1903, at Kitty Hawk, North Carolina, Orville and Wilbur Wright made the first sustained, controlled flights in a power-driven airplane. Their fourth and last flight of the day lasted 59 seconds and covered 852 feet.

Captain Barnaby: It was, but, on the other hand, I had built it and I had flown it, and I was already thinking about what the next one would look like. So that's how I got started into it, and then I did get associated with some of the model-flying boys in New York City. In 1909 we organized what I believe was the first model aero club in the U.S.A., called the New York Model Aero Club.

Q: They, indeed, were your contemporaries who were equally as enthusiastic.

Captain Barnaby: Yes, yes. And they include a number of men who have devoted their lives to aviation, like myself, and are still at it, although mostly retired now. I see a number of them from time to time, boys I was associated with in the New York Model Aero Club.

Q: Are they people with well-known names now in aviation?

Captain Barnaby: Well, in certain areas one of the best was a high school and college classmate of mine, Jean Roché, who was one of the original team that Colonel Clark got together in 1917 to form the original engineering division, which now is Wright-Patterson Air Force Base and that whole system.* Jean retired about five years ago. He was with the Air Force as one of their highest paid civilian engineers. He also was the designer and original president of the Aeronca Company and designed the early Aeroncas, which were very popular. I did some of his test flying for him back in 1928 and 1929, during the time that I was stationed out of Wright Field as liaison officer.

There are a number that I don't think of at the present time who are still in aviation or were until they retired. Then I began getting with other people interested in flying, and we built and flew a number of man-carrying gliders. That's how I knew Oakwood Heights down in Staten Island, because we used to keep our glider in Captain Baldwin's hangar, and we'd go down weekends and fly. That was Captain Tom Baldwin, the old balloonist and

---

* Colonel Virginius E. Clark, USA. Wright-Patterson Air Force Base, formerly Wright Field, near Dayton, Ohio, has the largest research and development center in the Air Force.

designer of the Army's first airship.* He, by the way, was a wonderful gentleman. He loved young people, witness the fact that he let us store our glider in his hangar down there and would always be ready with, "Are you sure you have enough carfare to get home?" and things like that. He looked after the boys. He was a wonderful man. I was very fond of him.

Then, aside from the glider fun and playing along, I didn't actually get into aviation until I'd finished college, of course.

Q: And college was Columbia?

Captain Barnaby: Columbia, yes.† I got my mechanical engineering degree there in 1915. It was during my senior year, I believe, that I was in some classes with Gene Wilson, naval officers' class of 1908.‡ There were a number of naval officers there, but Gene is the one that I knew best because we were together in the Bureau of Aeronautics for a number of years when he was heading up the power plant section.

Actually, my first job when I graduated from college was with the Elco Motor Boat Works in Bayonne, New Jersey. Engineering graduates had a pretty rough time back in those days. I went around applying for jobs, and I finally took the best offer I got, which was as a stockroom helper at the Elco Company for $11.00 a week.

Q: But I should think there would have been a spurt in employment and especially in the engineering field with World War I coming on.

---

* Captain Thomas Scott Baldwin, USA. The U.S. Army's first dirigible was tested and flown at Fort Myer, Virginia, in 1905 with Baldwin as pilot and Glenn H. Curtiss as engineer.
† Columbia University, New York City.
‡ Lieutenant (junior grade) Eugene E. Wilson, USN, who was involved in naval aviation until his resignation from the Navy in 1929. He became a civilian official and was president of United Aircraft Corporation in World War II.

Captain Barnaby: But, of course, you see, this was in '15, and we were in the neutrality kick at that time with Mr. Bryan as Secretary of State.* We were neutral, and there wasn't going to be any war. But it was while I was with the Elco Company that I met my first naval aviator, someone that I got to know very well much later. That was George Murray, USNA class of 1911, who died a few years ago as a retired vice admiral.†

The Elco Company was a subsidiary of the Electric Boat Company, which, of course, now is General Dynamics.‡ Knowing that I had some knowledge in aviation, they sent me up to New London to the Gallaudet aircraft plant to witness some flight tests of the Gallaudet seaplane.§ Gallaudet had been at Electric Boat seeking financing, and they wanted someone to tell them what he thought of the job and whether they should put money into it. So they sent me up there, and among the witnesses of these flight tests was Lieutenant George Murray, and he really was the first naval aviator I ever met. There also was an Army aviator acquaintance. Also among those present was Dusenberg, because two of his engines were in this Gallaudet seaplane. I had one of my early flights because I flew as observer on the first flights of this plane, flown by a test pilot, a Swede by the name of Bjorkland.

Q: Was it a single engine?

Captain Barnaby: No, it was a twin engine. It was a very far-out design. It had twin engines driving one propeller with a big ring gear, and the propeller was behind the wings. It was a pusher. The propeller was on a big drum rotating around the fuselage. It looked like the fuselage was cut in half.

---

* William Jennings Bryan was Secretary of State in the Wilson Administration from 1913 to 1915. The United States entered World War I in April 1917.
† Lieutenant (junior grade) George D. Murray, USN. Murray died in June 1956. He reached the rank of vice admiral on active duty and was promoted to four-star admiral upon retirement in August 1951.
‡ The Electric Boat Company of Groton, Connecticut, has long been one of the foremost builders of submarines for the U.S. Navy.
§ The Gallaudet Engineering Company produced two seaplanes for the U.S. Navy in the World War I era, the D-1 and D-4.

Q: Where were you seated? Out in front?

Captain Barnaby: Out in front, yes. I was in the front cockpit, and the pilot was behind me in the second cockpit.

Q: Could you really call it a cockpit? Weren't you right exposed to the . . . ?

Captain Barnaby: Oh, no, this was a closed cockpit. It was famous locally and in this country as being the first seaplane to cruise at over 100 miles an hour. The Navy was very interested in it. That was my first introduction to a naval aviator and an Army aviator, career men.

Q: They were rather rare people, weren't they?

Captain Barnaby: They were, yes. Let's see--that was in December 1916 that those test flights were made.

Q: Where would such naval aviators have been trained?

Captain Barnaby: Pensacola. You see, Pensacola was set up with Jack Towers in command in 1915, I believe.* He had the school at Pensacola. They had tents, tent hangars, they had their Wright machine on twin floats; they had the old Curtiss pushers. That was about it. But, of course, the first naval aviators, like Towers and Ellyson, trained up at Hammondsport, New York, at the Curtiss Company's school.†

Q: You were up at the Electric Boat.

---

* Lieutenant John H. Towers, USN, who was U.S. naval aviator number three. For a detailed biography, see Clark G. Reynolds, Admiral John H. Towers: The Struggle for Naval Air Supremacy (Annapolis: Naval Institute Press, 1991).
† On 19 January 1911, Lieutenant Theodore G. Ellyson, USN, became the first sduent at the flight school opened by Glenn Curtiss at North Island, Coronado, California. Later he was designated naval aviator number one.

Captain Barnaby: Yes. Well, because of structural problems and other problems, we nearly crashed because the rudder pedals collapsed during the flight. We had a pretty rough time, but we managed to get down and stay right side up.

Q: This was fairly usual on some of those early flights, wasn't it?

Captain Barnaby: Yes, and there were a number of design features that I didn't like about the plane. I didn't recommend that Electric Boat put any money into the Gallaudet Company, fond as I was of Edson Gallaudet, who was president of the company and a fine gentleman. I just didn't feel that he had the engineering staff that he needed at the time.

Q: Just a footnote, is that the same Gallaudet family that established the college for the deaf?*

Captain Barnaby: Yes, I'm sure it is.

There were two brothers. Edison I knew best. When I first met them in 1909, they were operating out of the old Mineola flying field on Long Island. There was a very early aviation center there at Mineola, Long Island, and then later it became famous as the takeoff site for the early transatlantic flights, including the Lindbergh flight.†

I left Elco in December of 1916, because my college classmate, Jean Roché that I mentioned earlier, was assistant chief engineer of the old Standard Aero Corporation in Plainfield, New Jersey. It was built around one Charles H. Day, who was one of the early airplane builders, and whose Day tractor was one of the early tractor biplanes.‡ By July 1917 aviation was starting to pick up because the war feeling was building up.§ So I left the Elco Boat Works and went over to Standard.

---

* Gallaudet College, Washington, D.C., named in honor of Thomas H. Gallaudet (1787-1851).
† Charles A. Lindbergh made the first solo flight across the Atlantic Ocean in May 1927.
‡ Depending on which way the engines were mounted, airplanes in that era were either "tractors," in which the engine pulled the plane, or "pushers."
§ The United States declared war on Germany on 6 April 1917.

Q: You say aviation was beginning to pick up. What vision did they have for aviation in case of war? What use?

Captain Barnaby: Well, the Army was flying airplanes. I think they were principally for observation then. Of course, you see, the war had been going on for two and a half to three years, and there was a fair amount of flying going on in connection with it.* The Germans, the British, and the French all had airplanes, and aviation was beginning to play some part in it. They'd even begun shooting at each other by that time, and a certain limited amount of bombing and ground strafing of troops and things of that kind.

Q: The German emphasis, at that period, was largely lighter-than-air craft, though, wasn't it?

Captain Barnaby: Yes, to a great extent. The Zeppelins.

Q: Remember the bombing raids over London?

Captain Barnaby: Oh, yes, yes, indeed, I stayed with Standard until the fall of 1917.
   Roché had left to go with the Army with Colonel Clark setting up the engineering division, which, by the way, started in the galvanized iron "Quonset Hut" building which is now part of the Smithsonian.

Q: Supposed to be temporary.

Captain Barnaby: Yes, temporary building in 1917 to house Colonel Clark's engineering division. That was the Colonel Clark who left his name in aviation as an airfoil designer. The Clark Y wing section was the most popular wing used, not only in this country, but

---

* The war in Europe started in August 1914.

also by the British. After the war, Colonel Clark left the Army. He and Reub Fleet went together and formed Consolidated Aircraft in Buffalo.*

Q: When you were with Standard Aero, what were they doing of interest?

Captain Barnaby: Along in the spring of 1917, they got an order for training planes. You see, in April war was declared. The War Production Board got going, and they standardized on training planes. There were to be two American training planes built. One was the famous Curtiss Jenny with the OX engine.† It was an eight-cylinder, V-type engine that Curtiss had developed for his racing motor cycles, it was a development from that. The other was the standard J-1 training plane, which was to utilize the Hall Scott A7A, four-cylinder, water-cooled engine. We at Standard went into production on the J-1s.

At that time I was assistant chief engineer, having taken Roché's job when he left. So I had to build up an engineering group and a group of designers and draftsmen to turn out production plans for this thing. The plans were then furnished to companies all over the country to build J-1 training planes.

Q: That was quite a project.

Captain Barnaby: There were hundreds of them built. It was quite a project, yes.

Q: What was the time factor in building a training plane?

Captain Barnaby: By the time I left, along towards November 1917, I would say that in our own plant we were turning out approximately one a day. Of course, they were being built

---

* Major Rueben H. Fleet resigned from the Army after World War I and was head of Consolidated Aircraft for many years. For a biography, see William Wagner, Reuben Fleet and the Story of Consolidated Aircraft (Fallbrook, California: Aero Publishers, 1976).

† This aircraft, one of the best known of the World War I era, got its nickname from the model designation JN.

in many places. I don't know how many, but it would number into the hundreds of the J-1 training planes.

Q: Was it an assembly-line technique?

Captain Barnaby: Oh, yes, and one of the big jobs that we had to do was to design and build the jigs and fixtures so that a wing built by the Lincoln Company would fit on a fuselage built by some other company.

Q: Standardized?

Captain Barnaby: Yes, standardized, and it was mass production. The components were all interchangeable, regardless of where they were built. At least, that was the intent.

Q: How closely did you have to work with the WPB?*

Captain Barnaby: I imagine very closely. I was just busy getting out the plans down there, and the external connections were above my scope.

Q: In the higher echelons?

Captain Barnaby: Yes, the higher echelons. I wasn't worried about that. The chief thing I was worrying about was keeping an engineering force together, because by the summer of 1917 the draft was beginning to pick them off.

Q: And they weren't exempted from the draft?

Captain Barnaby: We thought we were. We were assured by the president of the company that we would not be touched. But, one by one, the boys would be called, and they didn't

---

* WPB--War Production Board.

come back. Then the company began growing and bringing in management on top and on top. Finally, I decided I was going to get out and get into something a little closer to the war. I went to the post office and got an application for the Naval Reserve Flying Corps and also the aviation branch of the Army Signal Corps. I filled them out and sent them in, then sat back and waited to see which would answer first. The Navy answered first, and I was partway through ground school at MIT before I got an acknowledgement from the Army.* I told them they were too late; I was already in the Navy.

Q: And happily so?

Captain Barnaby: Happily so. Yes, I think so. Although I think I would have been happy either way.

Q: Just so it concerned flying.

Captain Barnaby: So long as it concerned flying, I'd have been happy either way. I wonder whether you would be interested in what part the Navy had in powerless flight, the gliding part of it?

Q: Yes, I would be very interested, and first I'd like to ask why the Navy was interested in gliders.

Captain Barnaby: It's hard to believe--although maybe not too hard to believe. Of course, as you know, the first Chief of the Bureau of Aeronautics was Admiral Moffett.† Admiral Moffett was a great believer in the power of publicity, and he felt that in order for the service to get anywhere--the part of the service he was interested in--you had to have the people on your side.

---

* MIT--Massachusetts Institute of Technology.
† Rear Admiral William A. Moffett, USN, was Chief of the Bureau of Aeronautics from July 1921 until his death in April 1933.

Q: The Congress?

Captain Barnaby: Yes, and the people, particularly as represented in Congress. He went in for things that would get favorable publicity for what he was doing and for what he thought the Navy should be doing, particularly in aviation. And I, having started in gliders, always was interested in them. As a sport I liked to fly the gliders.

Q: Had you maintained that simultaneously as you went along?

Captain Barnaby: Oh, yes, I kept up my glider-flying. Now, of course, you read now about these pilots with hundreds of thousands of flying hours. I'm not talking anything about that. If you had a few seconds of glider time, you were an expert.

Of course, in 1920 we began hearing about the German gliding schools and the things they were doing. It was in 1920 when Dr. Klemperer acquired the first soaring certificate over in Germany by making a flight of over an hour in his glider.* Of course, that intrigued all of us who had been interested in gliding from the start. From then on, gliding grew over there, and in 1928 some American industrialists, one of them being J.C. Penney, brought over some German glider pilots with their gliders, and they did some flying around the country.† A school was established on Cape Cod, at South Wellfleet, by an outfit called the American Motorless Aviation Corporation--AMAC.

Along in the spring of 1928, I had tried to get a month's leave from the Navy to go over to Germany to take a course in one of their glider schools, but I was turned down. So when I read in the spring of 1929 that there was this school up in Cape Cod, I decided to pool my leave and go up and take the course at Cape Cod, which I did. I was fortunate enough with my background and gliding experience to be the first one to fulfill the requirements and get what was the first American soaring certificate. My FAI soaring

___

* Dr. Otto Klemperer became the first licensed glider pilot in 1920.
† James C. Penney was the founder of the nationwide chain of retail stores that bear his name.

certificate issued by the National Aeronautics Association was Number 1, authenticated and signed by Orville Wright.

Q: This was accomplished through the teaching of the German pilots?

Captain Barnaby: By the German pilots on Cape Cod. The President of AMAC was General John F. O'Ryan, who was a well-known businessman in New York, a general in the First World War. One of the directors was Sumner Sewall, who was governor of Maine and died within the last five years.* So I acquired my first soaring certificate up there, and it got some publicity.

Along in the fall of 1929 Admiral Moffett sent for me, and I thought, "What have I done wrong now?"

But when I got in his office he said, "Sit down, Barnaby. Barnaby, do you think it would be possible to launch a glider from the Los Angeles?"† That sort of staggered me. Then he said, "I don't want an answer now. You think it over and come in and see me tomorrow. Think it over carefully, because if your answer is yes, you're going to do it."

Well, I didn't sleep much that night, but the next day I went up to see him and I told him, yes, I thought it was possible, and I would do it under certain conditions. One was that the Navy acquire for me the glider that I had used in making my soaring flights on Cape Cod.‡ Also, that I go to Lakehurst and supervise putting the launching gear in the airship.§ He said okay.

The gliding school had folded up by then, and I made arrangements with them for the Navy to buy this German glider.

---

* Sumner Sewall, who served as Republican Governor of Maine from 1941 to 1945, died on 25 January 1965.
† The rigid airship USS Los Angeles (ZR-3) was built in Germany for the United States under the terms of the Versailles Treaty. Commissioned a U.S. naval vessel on 25 November 1924, she was 658 feet long and 60 feet diameter.
‡ A photo of the glider appears on page 16 of Barnaby's book, Gliders and Gliding: Design, Principles, Structural Features, and Operation of Gliders and Soaring Planes (New York: Ronald Press Company, 1930).
§ Naval Air Station Lakehurst, New Jersey, the Navy's East Coast site for lighter-than-air operations.

Q: It hadn't been disposed of?

Captain Barnaby: No, no. They hadn't disposed of them. As a matter of fact, they still were in a state of flux. They didn't know what they were going to do, and I think they were glad to get the money. So the Navy bought this glider.

Q: How much did they have to pay for it?

Captain Barnaby: Frankly, I don't remember. I haven't the slightest idea. I would imagine maybe they might have paid $3,000 for it, something like that.

Q: What was your reason for wanting the one you had used up there?

Captain Barnaby: Because I'd got more time in that one than any other glider I'd ever flown, you see. The soaring flight, in which I'd gotten my soaring certificate, had lasted for 15 minutes and 6 seconds. That was an American record at that time, because it exceeded the flight that Orville Wright had made in 1911 of 9 minutes and 45 seconds. Then I had made several flights in it after that. Actually, I had become quite an expert, because by then I had nearly 20 minutes of gliding time in that glider, which was probably three-quarters of my total gliding time. So that was the reason for that.

So we got the glider down to Lakehurst. I went up, oh, the first of January 1930 to Lakehurst and stayed there to supervise the installation of the release gear. They already had the trapeze and gear for attaching the airplane to the airship. I don't recall whether they had actually done any hook-ons or launches with the airplanes at that time or not.* They may have done some.

Q: Similar to catapulting then, was that it?

---

* The Navy's rigid airships served for a time as flying aircraft carriers, able to launch and recover small fighter planes by means of a trapeze arrangement.

Captain Barnaby: No. It hung underneath when the ship was under way, and they would just release and fly away. And then they had the hook-on gear that they could come back and hook on. That had been designed, and I think they may have made some attachments for launches. Your naval aviation history would tell that. I used the basic equipment structure that they had under the <u>Los Angeles</u> to make a mounting to hold the glider.

Q: What height did you anticipate being released from, and at what speed, and that sort of thing? Had you worked that out?

Captain Barnaby: Oh, yes, I had worked that out. I knew what the normal gliding speed of a glider was, and I wanted to have that much airspeed showing on my airspeed indicator before they released me. The first lieutenant of the airship, the Los <u>Angeles</u>, was Lieutenant Cal Bolster, who was later as a rear admiral, Chief of the Office of Naval Research.* Cal and I designed the gear to hold the glider, and he actually operated the lanyard that released the glider.

Q: On a signal from you?

Captain Barnaby: Well, yes. I started the countdown, as it were. We got the things all ready, and you're asking about the altitude and the speed for release. I had been at Cape Cod in the middle of the summer of 1929, and then we brought the glider along in the fall and took it to Lakehurst and set it up there. So it was six months since I had flown it, and I wondered whether, maybe, I should make some test flights. The only way we could do it there at Lakehurst was by automobile tow, because there were no hills. I was afraid that maybe we would wreck it. So I decided that the best way to do was to set it up and leave it alone. We would release at a high enough altitude so that I had plenty of time to learn to fly it again on the way down. So we picked 3,000 feet as being high enough, and that was

---

* Lieutenant Calvin M. Bolster, Construction Corps, USN.

what the release height was set at. We picked the 31st of January as being the day. The weather reports were good, and I slept there and . . .

Q: Was it supposed to be over New Jersey?

Captain Barnaby: Yes, over the air station at Lakehurst. I'll never forget that morning. I was up at 5:00 o'clock, because at 6:00 o'clock they were going to walk the airship out of the hangar. It was 16 above zero at that time. Clear, crisp, beautiful day, but cold--bitter cold. The first hitch was they couldn't get the hangar doors open. The ice had frozen in around them, so actually it was considerably later--a couple of hours later--before they brought the airship out.

Q: Were there newspapermen about?

Captain Barnaby: Oh, yes, a lot of them. As a matter of fact, they had three blimps that accompanied us and flew along with us with newspaper reporters and movie cameras.

Q: Were they Goodyear blimps?

Captain Barnaby: Two of them were blimps that Goodyear had built for the Navy. The third one was the old ZMC-2, designed by Ralph Upson of the Detroit Aircraft Corporation. It was a non-rigid but had a thin aluminum skin instead of the usual fabric skin. That ship was quite a historic experiment.

Q: Was Admiral Moffett also present?

Captain Barnaby: No. Admiral Moffett at that time was attending the famous disarmament conference in London.* He was away, and Towers was assistant chief at the time and

---

* The conference led to the London Naval Treaty, signed in April 1930. It extended the terms of the 1922 Washington Naval Treaty for another five years and also established cruiser tonnage ratios for the United States, Great Britain, and Japan.

acting in his absence. After they'd finally walked the airship out and had it balanced and everything, then we attached the glider. For the takeoff, I didn't ride in the glider; I rode in the control car of the Los Angeles. We cruised around, went down over Atlantic City, climbing gradually until we got up to 3,000 feet. Then, as the dirigible headed back towards the air station, I went back amidships, and there was a ladder which I climbed down to get into the cockpit.

Q: You must have had to wear heavy clothing.

Captain Barnaby: Yes. I couldn't wear too much clothing, because there wasn't room enough in the cockpit for too much. I had on a summer flight suit and a leather jacket over that. Probably had a sweater on under the flying suit too.

When I was down in the cockpit, I could talk to Bolster, who was just up in the hatch above me. After I was all set, I asked him to tell the crew to go ahead with the ship. See, they'd stopped the engines while I was climbing down to make it a little easier for me. I wanted them to speed up the engines, and I would let him know when I was reading 40 miles an hour on my airspeed indicator. So it proceeded that way, and when I got my airspeed up to 40 knots, I told Cal to tell them to hold that speed till we got to where they wanted to launch me. Then, when they got over the station, they gave Cal the signal and he started a countdown and pulled the lanyard.

Q: What direction were the winds on that occasion?

Captain Barnaby: The wind was out of the west, and it was a light wind. I don't think there was more than, oh, 10 or 12 knots.

Q: That would have blown you towards the ocean, wouldn't it?

Captain Barnaby: Yes, but we were headed towards the station, headed into the wind, and I told Cal when to release me. I told him, "Okay, go ahead." He gave me a ten count and pulled the lanyard. You remember the first test flights of these supersonic X-15 planes that they experimented with out at Edwards Air Force Base. They were flown first as gliders without their engines.* They were released at 45,000 feet from under a B-52. Someone said, "You mean to say that they released this man in a plane that had never been flown before, with no power?"

I said, "Yes."

"It seems terrible. How do you think he'd feel?"

I said, "I think I know how he'd feel, because some 30 years ago I went through the same experience sitting in a glider with no power under the Los Angeles."

He said, "Well, what did you think about?"

I said, "I sat there thinking, 'How the hell did I ever let myself get maneuvered into this situation?'"

Actually, the instant I was released, I felt perfectly happy. The only thing was that I stuck the nose down and got away from under the ship, because there were two big 18-foot propellers out in front of me and two behind me that seemed kind of close. Actually, I had no worry because she dropped away fast. I leveled off possibly 100 feet below the ship, and then it was just a nice ride down, but awfully cold. It was about 13 minutes coming down, which added over 50% to my total flying time.

Q: Yes, I can see. You had 20 minutes total before this. What about the speed of the descent?

Captain Barnaby: Well, 13 minutes for 3,000 feet.

Q: That figures into how much miles per hour?

---

* The rocket-powered X-15, built by North American Aviation, was the fastest manned aircraft ever flown. It was first airborne in March 1959 but not released from the mother plane. The first independent flight, in June 1959, was made with the engines shut off. The first powered flight was on 17 September 1959. The X-15's highest speed was 4,534 miles per hour in October 1967; the highest altitude was 354,200 feet in August 1963.

Captain Barnaby: I don't know, that's too much arithmetic for me to figure in my head. I could have stayed up longer if I hadn't been so cold. I just flew at a comfortable gliding speed. I made no attempt to hunt out up-currents and try to soar.

Q: Why was it conducted in the middle of the winter? Why not wait for a nice balmy summer day?

Captain Barnaby: That's what the people said down at Kitty Hawk in 1963, on the 60th anniversary. It was about 20 above zero that day with a 20-knot wind blowing off the sea. "Why couldn't the Wrights have made their first flight in the summertime?" Things always seem to work out that way. Admiral Moffett had the idea in December and said, "Let's get to it and do it." That was the only reason.

Q: Was the Navy elated at the success of this flight?

Captain Barnaby: I think so. I think they were very pleased at the publicity they got from it. I had the whole cover sheet of the rotogravure section of The New York Times, than which there was none richer in those days.*

Q: That's right. Was it an experiment that was repeated?

Captain Barnaby: Yes. Only once. Again on the 4th of July down over Anacostia in Washington.

Q: Again with the Los Angeles?

Captain Barnaby: With the Los Angeles. Lieutenant Tex Settle, who was later Vice Admiral Settle and is now Vice Admiral Settle (Retired), was the pilot in that launching.†

---

* Barnaby's flight was reported in a front-page story in The New York Times, 1 February 1930.
† Lieutenant Thomas G. W. Settle, USN.

Q: Captain, getting back to my question which caused laughter on your part: why was the Navy interested in gliders in the first place? Was it only because of the publicity or what?

Captain Barnaby: Well, there was an idea--also Admiral Moffett's--that it could be put to a practical use. They carried on these large rigid airships a landing officer in case a landing was to be made at a place other than a Navy lighter-than-air base. I think that was true of all the rigid airships; even the German rigid airships carried a landing officer. It was customary for any airship that was going to land at a certain field away from a regular airship base. They'd fly over the field, and this officer would parachute down. It was his job to organize and direct a landing crew. By pre-arrangement, I guess they would get the fire department, the police department, the Boy Scouts, the Rotary Club, and whatnot. They would gather people, and it was his job to explain what the functions were, because handling one of these big rigid airships was a tremendous job, particularly if there was any wind running. Wind altered the time.

Q: I can appreciate that. I know what it was handling the Goodyear, a small one.

Captain Barnaby: Well, you can imagine one of these huge rigid ones. And it was the thought that possibly they could release the glider for this purpose. Say they'd be cruising along at 6,000 or 8,000 feet. This glider would have a flat glide angle and would be able to make good--even with some maneuvering--ten to one, anyway. So from 6,000 feet, you'd have ten miles to go. He could release and proceed on and land at the field in his glider without the airship having to make a pass over the field first. The airship could lay off until he would go down and land where he wanted, which wasn't always true with the parachutes in those days. Now they have the steerable parachutes that you can land pretty well where you want. He could go down, using the glider, and organize the landing crew, and that was the purpose.

Q: Then it is true that in a glider you can more or less choose your spot of landing?

Captain Barnaby: Oh, yes. With the modern gliders, which have gliding angles as high as 40 to 1, from a mile up, 5,000 feet up, you have a radius of 40 miles in which you can pick your landing field below. There are very few areas of 40 to 80 miles' diameter that you can't find someplace you can set down in.

Q: Maybe the Andes or somewhere.

Captain Barnaby: Yes. But even down in there, you can wind your way and go down in some of the valleys, hopefully. But you have all the control over your landing speed. When we were operating regularly during the war with our gliders, the operations officers at the airfields used to be very worried when a glider would come. They'd immediately go into emergency landing procedure, because here was something coming in with no power, and I had to tell them, "Look, just handle these like any other airplane. I can fit myself into any one of the traffic patterns you want, and if you don't want me to land on the runway, just say so, and I can land off on the grass at the side and not interfere with your traffic at all. I have the advantage over the rest of them. I can hear them, and I won't interfere with them."

Q: They didn't always believe this, however, did they?

Captain Barnaby: They didn't always believe it, but it was a fact. Well, that Los Angeles experiment was really the first of the Navy involvement with the glider as a military aircraft.

Q: The Navy never went on to actually attach them to the lighter-than-air craft, did they?

Captain Barnaby: No. That was the end of that experiment. The airships didn't last very long, and, of course, the later airships, the Akron and the Macon, carried aircraft aboard, which could do the same thing and much better.* You could send an airplane 50 miles or

---

* See the Naval Institute oral history of Rear Admiral Harold B. Miller, USN (Ret.), who flew the F9C Sparrowhawk fighter from the airships Akron (ZRS-4) and Macon (ZRS-5). The Akron was lost in a storm in 1933 and the Macon in 1935.

100 miles ahead of the airship to a field, and it could get there half a day in advance to make preparations. So there was no need for the glider.

Q: Did you have to make an official report on this particular experiment?

Captain Barnaby: Yes. I'm sure I did, although I don't recall much about it, but a compilation from the news service would be a report.

Q: Tell me, Captain, what is the intention and what is the purpose of the modern glider in the Navy today? I understand they've purchased a couple of new ones.

Captain Barnaby: Well, it is just to familiarize the modern pilot, particularly the modern test pilot. I imagine you're thinking about Captain Prichard's outfit at NAS Patuxent, at the Navy test pilots' school.*

Q: Yes, I am.

Captain Barnaby: After all, a glider is just an airplane with no power, and any time you have an engine failure you're in a glider. I started back in 1930 and from then on trying to sell that to the Navy. I tried to sell them into instituting a glider course at Pensacola, for two reasons. First of all, I felt that every pilot should know how to handle his aircraft if the engine went out, and that a basic course in gliding would give him more confidence in his ability to try to handle an aircraft than anything else.

Q: Although actually the circumstances are vastly different. When a motor has conked out, you have that weight to contend with.

---

* Captain Reuben P. Prichard, Jr., USN, was director of the Navy Test Pilot School at Naval Air Station, Patuxent River, Maryland.

Captain Barnaby: But they still glide, and the modern airplanes have a much cleaner design aerodynamically. They have a fairly flat glide. Actually, the feeling has always existed in Europe, where practically all commercial pilots are required to be glider pilots first. They feel that it's part of the basic training. I had many arguments back in the very early '30s down in the Bureau of Aeronautics on that subject. Particularly, I can remember, with Marc Mitscher, who was chief of the Flight Division of BuAer at the time.* But I never was able to sell him. He could see no use, no reason, for gliders. I said, "Commander, down at Annapolis I see they have a big fleet of sailboats down there, that every midshipman has to learn to sail. Why is that?"

He said, "Well, any man who goes to sea should know how to sail a boat, because sometime he may have to sail. You may be damaged or your ship may be sunk and maybe in a lifeboat, he's going to have to know how to sail."

Q: Precisely the answer you wanted.

Captain Barnaby: I said, "That's the same thing that happens any time an engine quits in an airplane." He couldn't see the analogy. Admiral King did, and it was Admiral King, when he was chief of the Bureau of Aeronautics, who finally decided that we should institute a glider-training course at Pensacola on an experimental basis.†

Q: This was optional, was it?

Captain Barnaby: No. The way it happened was this: I had given up trying to sell it as a means of improving the aviator's skill and so forth. I then tried to sell it as a quick means of evaluating the prospective student's adaptability to learning to fly. I worked out a two-week glider-training course. I said I could tell in two weeks whether a man was going to make an aviator or wasn't going to make an aviator. And it was on that basis: using it as an

---

* Commander Marc A. Mitscher, USN. As a flag officer in World War II Mitscher gained fame as commander of Task Force 58 during operations in the Pacific.
† Rear Admiral Ernest J. King, USN, served as Chief of the Bureau of Aeronautics from 3 May 1933 to 12 June 1936.

elimination course which could be installed around at these various reserve training bases around the country. Before you went to the expense of shipping a student down to Pensacola, starting him through, using up all the flying time, and then determining he wasn't flight material, you could give him a two weeks' course of glider training and determine whether he was going to make an aviator. On that basis, the Navy ordered four gliders purchased and sent to Pensacola.

At that time, a very fine glider had been developed in this country by Professor R. E. Franklin of the University of Michigan. It had become practically a standard glider used for training all around the country for glider clubs and so forth. We bought those gliders, and the first two of them were to be delivered in June of 1933. I was ordered down on temporary duty to instruct some instructors at Pensacola as glider instructors, to start an experiment on a glider training course there. I spent the month of June at Pensacola.

We ran into a snag. The instruction from BuAer was that four, I believe, of their regular naval aviator instructors were to be taught to be glider instructors by me. The instruction also said they were to be volunteers. When I arrived there, the commandant said, "Barnaby, I don't know what we're going to do. We put the notice on the bulletin board. It's been on the board now ever since we got it a couple of weeks ago, and we have received no volunteers." This was Captain Rufus Zogbaum, who was commandant at Pensacola.*

I said, "Captain, don't you do anything about it, except I would like to have it posted and also announced at weekly inspection and so forth, that on next Saturday at Corry Field there will be an exhibition of glider flying. Then let's see what happens." Well, two gliders came down over the road on trailers from Michigan, and the two fellows that brought them down were both glider pilots. They were University of Michigan students who had teamed to fly on the Franklin gliders up there, and, of course, I'd done a fair amount of flying with them at Elmira. We had these gliders set up, and the Franklin man who actually made the first flight was Wally Franklin, Dr. Franklin's younger brother.

They were auto-towed with a 500-foot manila towline, 3/8 diameter line. You can get up to 300 feet on a 500-foot line. He was cut loose, did some figure 8s, came back, and

---

* Captain Rufus S. Zogbaum, Jr., USN.

landed in front of the crowd. There was quite a decent crowd out there, because I think they were looking for blood. And he came in and made a nice landing. Then I got in, and I was towed off and made a few flights. Then after I came down to land, I said, "Well, anyone else like to try it?" and with that they started lining up. We had no trouble with volunteers after that. Four instructors were picked who volunteered to take the course.

Q: Were you helped any, sir, by the fact that as I recall in the early '30s, it was a time when vocational aptitude tests were coming into prominence? Did this whole idea help you?

Captain Barnaby: I'm sure it must have. There was considerable interest also expressed in it by the medical department down there because they had a series of psychological tests. They were picking them out on the basis of psychological tests, and we were very interested in comparing notes. I think while I was down there during that first month, I trained two instructors. Then I went back to my job. I was inspector of naval aircraft at Glenn Martin's plant in Baltimore.

The first two trained four more men to be instructors. Then, the following June, '34, I was ordered to Pensacola to be the assembly and repair officer, with additional duty of supervising the glider course. Beginning with the student class that was due to arrive on the first of July, it was arranged that the first half of that class, which I believe was about 20 students, were to come two weeks early. They would get the glider training course, then proceed on with the rest of their class who would arrive two weeks later.

I think classes were coming about every three months at that time. After these men had finished their two weeks' glider-training course--if they finished, because some of them they grounded for their own safety--the instructor's job was to rate each student. He had ratings of superior, above average, average, below average, inferior, and "He'll kill himself" when they didn't even want him to finish the glider course. These records were kept confidential. They did not go on to the flight instructors.

The whole class of 40 students went to the regular flight school, and then proceeded on through the flight course. Then at the end we tried to compare their flight records through the flight school, which at that time lasted pretty close to a year. They started in primary seaplanes, and they got trained in everything, right up through the big flying boats to the carrier fighters, the whole works. Later on, when the wartime speedup started, they started splitting them off. There were carrier pilots and the big-boat pilots, but in those days you got the full treatment.

The results, I think, confirmed my feeling in the thing, that we could predict flying aptitude. The records are available in BuAer buried somewhere, but I also had a copy of the report.

Q: How long were they continued?

Captain Barnaby: That lasted about a year.

Q: Why did they discontinue them?

Captain Barnaby: The war came on, and they didn't have time to waste with it. I saw the final report from Pensacola that went to BuAer giving the results and telling how they compared with the flight course. I forget what the total number of students that went through the glider course was, maybe around 50. Of those who did average and above on the glider course, only two failed to pass the flight course. Of those rated inferior and impossible, about the same proportion, about 2 of them passed the flight test. And in comparing them with the psychological tests they were pretty good, too, although I think the glider-training hit it a little closer than they did, which I would have expected. On the report that got to BuAer, one of the endorsements to it is Admiral King's note "Something should be done about this. EJK."

Q: What was his interest?

Captain Barnaby: His intent was that it be continued, and on top of that was a note "File this." It went in the files, and that was the end of it.

Q: Were there any casualties in that time?

Captain Barnaby: There were no fatalities. There were a number of casualties, yes. We had a number of crashes. Of course, the casualties to gliders were considerable; we'd bust them up now and then. Of course, that was my headache, because I had the overhaul shops. We started with six gliders, and we finished with six gliders, but some of them that were flying had an awful lot of parts that weren't in the original gliders. I was practically manufacturing them to keep them going. We wrecked a lot of gliders.

Q: You say, Captain, that simultaneously, and continuing, this is a part of European training?

Captain Barnaby: That is my understanding. Of course, the whole Luftwaffe was built up from their glider training in the '30s through to 1939 and on. And there was no more gliding in the Navy after that until the war came along and until the Germans startled the world with using them as military transports. They used gliders first in the invasion of the low lands and of Crete and then later in Norway. That, of course, started a whole glider program, the big one that the Army Air Corps had and much later, the less ambitious one that the Navy started.*

Q: That was the kind of publicity, the kind of spectacular which got us interested.

Captain Barnaby: The only thing it appears that can get something started in this country is to have someone else do it. I mean, you couldn't get our military services interested in the rotary wing until the Germans started using helicopters in the war. They, the enemy, were the best salesmen.

Q: Very interesting point.

---

* On 20 July 1941 the U.S. Army Air Corps was officially redesignated the U.S. Army Air Forces.

Captain Barnaby: It's interesting but kind of sad, I think, that we always have to be waiting for someone else. After all, the aircraft carrier was a British invention.

Q: How do you explain this factor?

Captain Barnaby: I don't try to explain it. I don't know. It's just something that seems to be true. Of course, the space program is like that. And back ahead of that, the whole rocket business, the long-range bombs started with the buzz bombs, V-1s and then later the V-2s bombed London and were the very beginning of our space program.

Q: And Dr. Goddard didn't get very far, did he?*

Captain Barnaby: He didn't get very far.

Q: And I can think of another illustration--radar. It was the Battle of Britain which put it on the map.

Captain Barnaby: It put it on the map, and I think it was radar and the tenacity and the obstinacy of the RAF who just would not be licked that made the Battle of Britain come out the way it did.† Those fighters that Winston Churchill made the famous remark about that they just would not be licked, and the radar to help them, turned the tide there. Later, just before we got in the war, before Pearl Harbor, the Navy again started an interest in gliders for military purposes. At that time I was at the Naval Aircraft Factory.‡ I don't remember whether I was chief engineer or assistant chief engineer at the time we got our first directives from BuAer.

---

* American scientist Robert H. Goddard did pioneering research work with rockets in the 1930s.
† RAF--Royal Air Force.
‡ The Naval Aircraft Factory was at Philadelphia. For a history of the factory that contains a number of mentions of Captain Barnaby, see William F. Trimble, Wings for the Navy: A History of the Naval Aircraft Factory, 1917-1956 (Annapolis: Naval Institute Press, 1990).

Q: Were you instrumental in reviving this?

Captain Barnaby: I don't know whether I was or not. I think I may have had some hand in it. I talked it wherever I could and certainly as soon as I got all the facts as to what the Germans were doing, and I tried to keep informed.

But I was in Philadelphia, at the aircraft factory, when we got our first directives to do design studies on military gliders. They had two primary purposes in mind. One was for the Marines to use in their island-hopping program in the Pacific, cleaning the Japs out of the islands as they advanced. The other thing was as a means of transporting large packages. For instance, the largest radial engines, the big Pratt & Whitney and Wright, multi-bank radial engines that were being used on our big flying boats, could not be transported by aircraft; they couldn't get them in the airplanes.

So the specifications for the first gliders we built were that they should have the capacity and have a hatch big enough to load one of these R-2250 or R-2270 engines--I forget which--and be able to carry it as cargo. The other was to be able to carry ten fully-equipped Marine troops or a machine gun and crew and ammunition. And the gliders were to be amphibious, the idea being they would take off, be towed off _from_ a flying field, but would go in and land on the water just outside the surf and plow right in through the surf and up onto the beach, and there they were expendable. They'd run them up on the beach and unload their troops and their machine guns and whatnot.

Q: How far were they anticipated to fly before landing on the beach?

Captain Barnaby: Well, they would like to be able to launch them far enough away so that the tow planes would not be subjected to antiaircraft batteries.

Q: I see, out beyond the range.

Captain Barnaby: Out beyond that, or if not beyond the range, beyond the visual range on shore so that they could turn them loose before they got shot at. For instance, at night, they could come in fairly close until their sound would do it; at least they would not have to come all the way in. Then turn these gliders loose with sufficient altitude so that their glide angle with the wind direction and so forth would make sure that they could reach the beach and could run them onto it.

Q: One of their chief virtues was the fact that they were expendable, and also they were silent.

Captain Barnaby: That's right. And, being expendable, they were not too expensive as compared with the comparable airplane. We developed designs, contracts for them were let, and gliders were built. But by the time we really got into production and were starting to deliver gliders, the war had advanced so far that they were not needed.

Q: Were people like Kelly Turner really interested in this?*

Captain Barnaby: I don't think so, not to any great extent. I think that it was one of those things that they were pushed into reluctantly, although I don't blame them for that. The whole history of military development was that way. You know how the old Navy fought the carrier and aviation in general. I think it was Admiral C. F. Hughes who volunteered to go out and stand on the deck during General Mitchell's bombings off the coast there.†

Q: Yes.

Captain Barnaby: There was no finer gentleman than Rear Admiral Hughes; I knew him well. He was commandant of the naval district there in Philadelphia when I first went to the

---

* Vice Admiral Richmond Kelly Turner, USN, was one of the Navy's principal amphibious commanders during the Pacific War.
† In June 1921 Brigadier General William Mitchell, USA, Chief of the Army Air Service, supervised the bombing off the Virginia Capes of the formerly German battleship <u>Ostfriesland</u>. The Army bombers sank her on 21 June. Rear Admiral Charles F. Hughes, USN, was a battleship division commander in 1921. As a four-star admiral, he served as Chief of Naval Operations from 1927 to 1930.

Naval Aircraft Factory in 1920; that was my first tour there.* I tried to inject the aviation bug into him, but his hide was a little too thick. Every new development has to be forced on the services. My gosh, think of the parachute. You were a sissy to wear a parachute. I remember very well when the orders came out back in the '20s that every naval aviator would have a parachute on. The original order didn't say that they had to wear it, so they sat on them but wouldn't put the harnesses on.

Q: Pretty much the same with the safety belt in the car, isn't it?

Captain Barnaby: Yes, you just can't get them to do it. Of course, I was not myself particularly enthusiastic about the glider as a military weapon. I think that it proved to be a pretty costly experiment. Goodness knows, the casualties were very high in the Normandy landings. It worked fine for the Germans, because no one was expecting it. The element of surprise worked in that case, but it never worked again and it didn't work when the Normandy invasion took place.† They used a great many gliders.

Q: They were used extensively.

Captain Barnaby: Oh, yes, not in the initial landing but within the next 24 hours and so forth. After the initial D-Day attack, a large number of troops, particularly the British, were taken over to the continent by glider. By that time, the Germans knew the invasion was coming; the only thing they didn't know was where.

---

* Hughes served as Commandant of the Fourth Naval District and Philadelphia Navy Yard from 1918 to 1920.
† As part of the Allied invasion of Normandy on 6 June 1944, both British and American glider units put troops ashore in France, using a total of about 850 gliders. Despite relatively high casualty rates among pilots and passengers, the gliders made a substantial contribution to the opening phase of the Normandy campaign.

From reading all the books that have been written since, it appears that that was the only thing that made it succeed, because the German high command still thought the Normandy invasion was just a feint. They thought that the real attack was going to come up at Pas de Calais, and they wouldn't move the troops down. Rommel was screaming for them down there, but they still thought it was a feint until too late.* But they did know an attack was coming, and all the fields that they thought might be used for glider landings were booby-trapped. I mean they planted posts all over these fields. With a post-hole digger they just put in these posts about three feet high and to land in among those just tore the glider to pieces and lots of troops were lost in the landings.

To be of any value, you've got to get them down on the ground and get the people out of them. The idea was fine, and, under ideal conditions, it was great, because you could get a group of men in together with their equipment. Whereas with paratroops you distribute them over the countryside, and then their first job is to try and reassemble, and out go with machine guns and artillery of one kind or another, and packages of ammunition, and it's strewed all over the countryside. But with the glider, you'd have a complete unit ready to go if you got it down. You also lost a complete unit if you didn't get it down.

Q: Why did the British use it more extensively than we did in the Normandy landings?

Captain Barnaby: Well, they just had more gliders, and that was part of their operation. I don't know if it was a tactical decision of who did what. Of course, we had a glider invasion from North Africa into Sicily and Italy earlier, which was rather catastrophic too.

I've always felt that there were two reasons why the glider programs were not a success. The first and basic one was that the term "glider" ever got into the act at all, because it meant that when they decided to go into it, they went to the glider people for their knowledge of design of gliders and use of gliders and so forth, rather than going to the airplane people. Because actually they're not gliders as we thought of gliders; they're towed airplanes. The basic difference is that a glider must spend as little time as possible on the

---

* Field Marshal Erwin Rommel was commander of the German defense force at Normandy.

towline, and then spend its time flying round on rising currents and soaring and so forth. That's the glider program as it was before and as it is now as a sport. The military glider pilot spends most of his life on the end of a towline, getting to his objective. When he cuts loose, his object is to get on the ground as fast as possible, because as long as he's in the air he's a sitting duck.

Q: And most often, no intention of retrieving the plane.

Captain Barnaby: No intention of retrieving. The whole concept was different. When the glider's in tow, that's the uncomfortable part of the ride in the normal soaring glider. As a matter of fact, during all my glider-flying days, I never entered in my logbook the time I was on tow, because I wasn't glider-flying.

Q: That was just a means to an end.

Captain Barnaby: That was the means to getting up there. I started my time when I pulled the release and was on my own.

Q: The use of gliders in military operations--was the Army concept any different from the Navy, or was it a joint operation and a dual . . . ?

Captain Barnaby: The concept was very much the same. The only thing was that our whole program was for the Marines, and they were all amphibious gliders. They were all waterborne.

Q: They all had pontoons?

Captain Barnaby: They were like flying boats. They had to be amphibious, because you used land-based tow planes. They towed off from the land, and thereafter they cranked up their wheels or jettisoned them and planned to land in the water.

Q: Had there been a hiatus in the military use of gliders until the present time, or what?

Captain Barnaby: Yes, as far as the Navy is concerned, things ended after the school at Pensacola, which finished up when the cadet training program started in 1935 and when they started pushing students through in mass production.* Then they had a class coming in with 100 every month or something like that--the cadet drive. There was no gliding in the Navy officially until this purchase of gliders down at the school at Patuxent.

Q: Was this envisioned as something of a continuation of what was . . . ?

Captain Barnaby: No. I haven't had a chance to talk with Captain Prichard, and I don't know how it got started. I didn't know it was started until after the gliders were down there. I had a letter from a gliding friend of mine, saying, "You'll be interested to know that the Navy has bought some soaring planes for the test pilots' school at Patuxent, and they're going to use them as part of their training for test pilots."

Before I had a chance to start investigating, out of the clear blue I had a telephone call from Captain Prichard one day saying, "You probably don't know, but we have got some gliders down here and we're flying them. We'd like to have you come down and visit us and see what we're doing."†

I said, "Well, as a matter of fact, if you'd called me up last week, I would have had to say, no, I didn't know, but I got a letter just the other day telling me that you had gliders down there." At that time I told him I hoped to be down the last of June at the Golden

---

* The AvCad--aviation cadet--program was instituted in 1935. Under this program individuals enlisted in the Naval Reserve, then were trained as aviators and sent to the fleet in cadet status until later being commissioned as officers. In 1939 the program was modified so that individuals were commissioned upon successful completion of flight training.

† See Commander J. A. Pursch, MC, USN, "Daedulus and Icarus of Patuxent River," Naval Aviation News, April 1970, pages 6-13.

Eagles' reunion.* Then later I had to call him up and tell him I was sorry I wouldn't make it, but that I would hope to get down and see him some time later in the year. I said that I was very anxious to see him, because the largest glider that the Navy ever built was assembled and test-flew down there at Patuxent, as having the longest naval runway in the area.

Q: Well, I hope you get there, because Captain Prichard is a very enthusiastic man.

Captain Barnaby: I gather so.

Q: He's a go-go person, I gather.

Captain Barnaby: I think it's very interesting, because I still go back to the sailboat analogy, that when the engine quits in an airplane you're in a glider. Nothing makes me feel sadder than the apparent doctrine that when your engine quits in the modern airplane, you bail out. Now, I can see the difference between those airplanes and the gliders that I have been flying around in, landing speed being one, and you don't settle down in the nearest pasture or cornfield, but it does seem to me and it has been proved by the work they do out at Edwards Air Force Base, that it is possible, if you have the room, to set an airplane down with no power.

Q: Captain, I think it might be a good idea, since you've been talking about the military aspects of the glider, that you might, as something of a corollary, tell me about the development of these meets at Elmira in New York and your participation in them because I suspect you had.

Captain Barnaby: Yes, I'd be glad to do that. Of course, having been so fortunate as to acquire the first soaring certificate in the United States, I immediately became "old man

---

* The Golden Eagles is a group of naval aviators who have been in the profession for many years and made substantial contributions.

soaring" himself, though I had maybe only 15 or 20 minutes of soaring time. I was immediately invited to become a director of the National Glider Association, as it was then. When they held the first glider meet up at Elmira in 1930, why, I was a guest there, and was invited to fly the various gliders that were present. Little did they know how little I knew about it, but I guess I knew as much as anyone else.

The National Glider Association ran the first two contests, the '30 and '31 contests, and then it folded up due to financial difficulties and one thing or another. In the spring of '32, it was decided that if we were going to have another contest, other steps would have to be taken. A group of us was headed by Warren Eaton of Norwich, New York. He was one of the Eaton family who founded Norwich Pharmaceutical Company--Unguentine and Pepto Bismol and such things. There were three brothers. I guess the company had been founded by their father, but there were three brothers: Robert Eaton, Mel Eaton, and Warren was the youngest brother. Mel Eaton was Republican chairman for the state of New York for a goodly number of years and president of the Norwich Pharmaceutical Company. Well, Warren Eaton was the spark plug in getting together a group, and in the spring of 1932, the Soaring Society of America was formed for the purpose of holding a national contest in the summer of 1932 at Elmira.

The Soaring Society started off with a membership of less than 100; they're now up around 10,000 and growing fast. The curve is on an upward sweep. A couple of years ago I wrote an article for the Soaring Magazine, which is the organ the Soaring Society puts out. I had run across my ledger book, because when I was stationed in Pensacola in 1935, I was president and acting treasurer of the Soaring Society in 1935, '36, '37. I took over the job from Warren Eaton, who was killed in a glider accident. I had the ledger there, and in 1936 we had 170-some members and our income for that year was around $900.00. I compared it with the 1967 budget, which was $90,000.

Q: My heavens.

Captain Barnaby: They have a paid general secretary, and a paid editor, a paid staff, and around 10,000 members.

Q: Great oaks from little acorns, isn't it?

Captain Barnaby: Isn't that the truth? But all of the contests up until after World War II were held at Elmira. Lots of people ask why Elmira. Well, when we got started going over here in the '30s, particularly after this German team had come over and run the school at Cape Cod and things started to build up--it was also the time that Goodyear brought over a lot of the zeppelin engineers who started Goodyear Aviation and with the contract to build the Akron and the Macon. Among those was the man who had achieved the first German soaring certificate, Dr. Wolfgang Klemperer who, incidentally, is a cousin of . . .

Q: Otto, the conductor?

Captain Barnaby: The conductor, Otto Klemperer, and who was a Gotha pilot in World War I and bombed England.

Well, Dr. Klemperer came over to the Goodyear-Zeppelin Company, and some of our glider people got in touch with him. A number of sites had been suggested around the country as a possible soaring center similar to the one in Germany at the Wasserkuppe. He volunteered to go and look over these sites and pick one. The site he picked was Elmira, because there were the broad, flat valleys, mostly under cultivation or pasture land, and the ridges, the hills, with plateaus and cleared places on the top. It more nearly resembled that part of Germany where they had their soaring school there. He in the spring of 1930 selected Elmira. Also, Elmira was a fairly good-sized town and had a couple of hotels and facilities that could support us and things like that. It was industrial.

Q: And a pleasant climate.

Captain Barnaby: And a very pleasant climate. And one of the pioneer glider pilots by the name of Jack O'Meara took his glider up there in the early summer of 1930, made a couple of soaring flights, one of four hours. That cinched Elmira for the first national soaring contest, which was held in late August or early September of 1930. They held a contest there every year up until--they were not held in '42, '43, '44, and '45, but in '46 we had one up there. I was again president. In fact, I'm the only five-time president of the Soaring Society. By then we had discovered that soaring didn't have to be associated with hills. We discovered the thermal concept--the thermals, as they called it--the heating of the air by the sun.

Q: You'd been observing more closely the hawks then, in the mountains?

Captain Barnaby: Well, yes, and actually it was a German soaring pilot, Wolf Hirth, who in 1930 recognized and named the thermal currents. Still, even then, it took several years before people would venture away from the hills. So the next contest, in '47, was held down in the broad flatlands of Texas at Wichita Falls, at the mothballed Air Corps base down there, which is now activated again.* We held a very successful soaring contest there, and since that time, they've been held all over the country, like Elsinore, California, McCook, Nebraska. But every now and then, they'd come back to Elmira and, as a matter of fact, in 1968 the contest was at Elmira.

For a number of years they didn't have it at Elmira, because the site of the contest outgrew the sites up there. It took a little political pressure and so forth to get the county and New York State to put a little more money into the soaring sites. They finally got it back again last year, and held a very fine contest. Marg and I stopped there over the 4th of July on our way up here from Philadelphia to watch the soaring. Elmira is sparkplugged by the presence of the Schweitzer Aircraft Corporation, which is the only real manufacturing company that produces sailplanes in quantity. Incidentally, the sailplanes which they have down at Patuxent are Schweitzers.† But that's how come Elmira has maintained. We

---

* Sheppard Air Force Base.
† The plane, designated QT-2PC, was a Lockheed-modified Schweitzer SGS 2-32 sailplane with a 100-horsepower Continental reciprocating engine. For a photo, see <u>Naval Aviation News</u>, December 1969, page 26.

thought we were going to lose it for a while, but it got more speed again. It's now been known since 1930 as the glider capital of America. They are jealous of that.

Q: Well, I think in the eyes of the public, Elmira is associated with gliding and always has been.

Captain Barnaby: Yes, and it all results from the survey that Dr. Klemperer made. Dr. Klemperer left Goodyear when they got out of the aircraft business, and was director of research for Don Douglas out at Douglas Aircraft.* He died about five years ago. His birthday was two days ahead of mine.

Soaring as a sport has grown and grown. The records are just unbelievable to people who haven't been wrapped up in it. People will say, "How long can you stay up?" The Federation Aeronautique International, the FAI, is the international body which promulgates and authenticates all of the national and international records; it's like the sporting organizations. Over ten years ago, the FAI by unanimous vote struck duration from the list of records, because some Frenchman doped himself up and made a flight of 60 hours. Then he tried to exceed that, and they found him dead in the wreckage of his glider because he overdosed himself to stay awake. So they decided that duration was just a form of flagpole-sitting and had nothing to do with science or sport. But distance is still of importance, and the United States holds the distance record. It's something over 600 miles--from down in Texas to up in one of the northwestern states.

Q: Would initial height have any bearing at all?

Captain Barnaby: No, no bearing whatsoever. As a matter of fact, it's apt to detract. Well, on a 600-mile flight it wouldn't make any difference, but they subtract what you could glide from your release point without any up currents, for instance, from the total distance. It's

---

* Donald W. Douglas was the founder and long-time head of Douglas Aircraft Company, which has since become part of the McDonnell Douglas Corporation.

got to be soaring; you've got to be keeping yourself up by pulling on your bootstraps, so to speak.

Q: Otherwise they'd be cheating when somebody goes 50,000 feet.

Captain Barnaby: Well, that wouldn't be enough even at 50,000 feet. That's ten miles, and that would only be 400 miles, or something like that, the most you could make. You couldn't break the record at that rate. So what the pilot does, he gets towed up, and the tow pilot knows where he wants to go and where he thinks the lift is. The tow pilot can tell that if the tow plane suddenly starts to rise, it's hit some rising air. As soon as it hits him, he'll release. The lower he can release, the better because there is less to subtract from his total distance. But, as I say, distance over 600 miles--and now that's getting to the point where people are losing interest in the straight distance, because you know you're going to have to come down when the sun goes down. First of all, all the thermal activity dies very quickly after that.

Q: It's dependent on the sun, is it?

Captain Barnaby: Yes. The heating of the ground, and the air above it starts boiling up. Then, the other thing is you've got to be able to see where you're going and see where you're going to set down. After dark you'd be kind of hard-pressed to find a landing site to go into.

Q: Captain, you spoke before, when you were talking about the military aspects of gliding and the possibility of use for landing on beaches at night.

Captain Barnaby: Well, I don't think they planned to do it at night. They might make their approaches just before dawn with the idea that by the time they had cut loose and started on the glide in that there would be enough daylight for them to land by.

Q: I was thinking in terms of the activity of the sun.

Captain Barnaby: Oh, the military glider doesn't worry about that. First of all, their normal sinking speed is so great that it's not going to make any difference to them. That's another reason that they have so little relationship to the soaring machine. It's possible with the military gliders we experimented on, with a light load, and on a good day, to soar them. For instance, one of our amphibious Navy gliders, I was out one day with it to do some test flying and also taking some of my boys that wanted to ride along. I think I had six sailors with me, and we cut loose over the field at Johnsville, a naval air development center above Philadelphia. I found enough current, and we cut loose at 2,000 feet, and I climbed it up to 3,000 feet, and we flew around for over half an hour before we came in and landed. But that's unusual, and it was lightly loaded, as opposed to its military function. Of course, they worried about wind direction, because that would determine the speediness of your glide and how far you're going to get, because if the wind was as great as your glide speed and you tried to go into it, you aren't going to go anywhere except straight down.

Q: Yes.

Captain Barnaby: However, if you turned downwind, you'd go a long way.

There are some interesting things I wanted to mention in connection with our glider work at the Naval Aircraft Factory and later up at Johnsville, where I was the first commanding officer when the Navy took over. It was the Brewster Aeronautical Company's plant, and the Navy took it over on the first of July 1944. It was then known as the Naval Air Modification Unit.

I had a group of Marine officers as test pilots. One day Major Dick Figley was on a cross-country flight and had an oil-line failure.* The engine didn't burn up, but it seized and quit, and he had to make a forced landing. He was flying over Akron at the time and he set down there. It was a single-engine plane; I believe it was an SB2U, which is a scout

---

* Major Richard E. Figley, USMC.

bomber built by Vought. He telephoned in and said he was down there with a stuck piston. What should he do? It seemed that the only thing to do was either to send a crew out there with a new engine and change engines out there, or to send a truck out and take the wings off the airplane, and truck it back. Then someone in my group had a bright idea and said, "Why don't we tow him back?"

That sounded like a good idea, and I got him on the telephone again out there at Goodyear and said, "Dick, how about we send our Tugboat Annie out there and tow you home?"

He said, "Do you think you can do it?"

I said, "Well, we have another SB2U here. We'll try it here and if it works all right, why, we'll come out and get you."

Q: What was the weight of a plane like that?

Captain Barnaby: I would say 10,000 or 12,000 pounds. So we took this airplane, took the propeller off, and rigged a towline fitting on the engine shaft hub. We had a release hook, with a lanyard back to the cockpit, and one of our Marine aviator glider pilots was in the plane being towed. We towed him behind the Tugboat Annie, which was a Consolidated PBY amphibian. We towed him off the field, towed him around a while, and then he cut loose and brought it in, landing on the field. "That flies fine," he said. So we called Figley back and said, "It works fine, flies fine. You get the propeller off and we'll bring a tow fitting out for you." We went out and hooked on to him, and brought him home in about two hours from out there.

Q: Amazing. Had this ever been done before?

Captain Barnaby: Never been done before. Then another one of our planes, a twin-engine Grumman amphibian, had an engine go bad. He landed at the Marine base on Manteo, North Carolina, which is down near Kitty Hawk, one of the islands in the sound there, and we towed him home.

From then on, we would get calls from various places: "We got a plane down somewhere with a bent prop or something like that, can you tow us in?" So we organized what we called the NAMU towing service, and from that came the idea of towing fighters to extend their range. You see one of the troubles was on the continent when they began getting the big bombers, that they couldn't have fighter protection all the way into Germany and out again because the fighter planes at that time didn't have the range. So we had the idea that we could take fighters and tow them, say, in the formation of bombers. You'd take a bomber and instead of loading it with bombs, give it plenty of fuel and let it tow a fighter, or tow two fighters.

Q: You mean end to end?

Captain Barnaby: No, we'd tow them on two towlines, sort of fan arrangement. We did that with gliders; we'd tow two and three. As a matter of fact, I have seen as many as six in tow.

Q: Sort of air freight idea.

Captain Barnaby: Yes. We ran some air freight experiments, too, for towing gliders. And we conducted experiments. We towed two fighters behind a B-17 which I borrowed from the Army Air Corps, as it was then. They went for ten hours over a triangular course from Philadelphia, to Patuxent, to Atlantic City and back, just towing them round and round to see whether it was more fatiguing riding that way on the end of a towline than flying. We made some long tows. There again, it was a bright idea but it came too late, because they shortly developed this idea of the fighters carrying auxiliary wing tanks that they could drop. When they got out to the combat area, they would use the fuel out of those tanks. Then they'd jettison those tanks and be able to do their fighting and have enough fuel to get home.

Q: Was the idea entertained in connection with ferrying fighters across the ocean?

Captain Barnaby: Yes, but there again they reached the point where they could use the belly tanks. The first ferries were, I think, from Natal to Dakar across the South Atlantic, and they could do that. But there was some towing. I remember the Air Corps made quite a bit of the fact they towed some of these little liaison planes, like Piper Cub type of planes that they used for this low-altitude liaison, by towing some of those from some base down in the South Pacific a couple of thousand miles to someplace else during the war. We did some towing of that kind. But that was an interesting development of the glider business.

Q: Yes, indeed it was, and it has, as you say, been superseded now.

Captain Barnaby: Yes. There are other things that come along, just like I don't think there'll be any more military gliders. Then another development was the glide-bomb, which was just a glider carrying a bomb load.

Q: This was the German idea, wasn't it?

Captain Barnaby: Well, they had some, but we also had some at the same time, and ours got to quite sizable proportions. For instance, we had developed, there at the Naval Aircraft Factory, pilotless aircraft. These were the airplanes which flew by themselves and were controlled remotely. It was done by Admiral Fahrney, who was a captain back in those days.* He had been interested for years in the radio control. The idea was to fly these things into targets, and we had a design like an airplane or a glider. They were more like airplanes without any engines in them, and they'd carry a 2,000-pound bomb. They had a television camera in the nose, and the mother plane that towed them out to within glide distance of the target, and then it would release the glider. They would guide it by the

---

* The concept of using attack drones configured to deliver weapons by remote control was a distant forerunner of the guided missile concept. See Rear Admiral Delmar S. Fahrney, USN (Ret.), "The Birth of Guided Missiles," U.S. Naval Institute Proceedings, December 1980, pages 54-60.

picture in the scope toward the target. At that time of World War II, one of the big problems was the submarine pens at Ostend because they would tunnel back into the hills and they found that dropping bombs on them did no good at all. They had plenty of mountain above to take the load.

Q: Also at St. Nazaire, weren't they?

Captain Barnaby: Yes, there were a number of places along there. The thought was that they'd make some of these big glide bombs, bring them over, and guide them by television, and fly them into the mouths of these tunnels. The Air Force contributed a flock of Liberator B-24s, and they came down to Philadelphia and we put in the radio-control equipment and the television, which we had developed in cooperation with RCA.* We put the receiving and control equipment in the mother planes, and they went over to England. But the English balked on taking these airplanes out of their fields with no pilots in them, with remote control, carrying a load of 24,000 pounds of TNT. And you can't blame them.

Q: Because it was over the countryside.

Captain Barnaby: Because they had to go across miles of countryside before they got to the coast to head on across the North Sea to their target.

Q: Couldn't that objection have been met by fields near the coast?

Captain Barnaby: They didn't have any suitable, because this required an extremely long field. Then there was a time factor in making a field. So the decision was that they would call for a volunteer pilot and copilot, who would take them off, then on their way to the coast, the mother plane would check out the control system, put it on automatic control, and they would fly it and so forth. Then, when everything was squared away, these men

---

* RCA--Radio Corporation of America.

would bail out before they got to the coast line, and the plane would proceed on its way. Well, the first plane to take off, the first trial plane, was piloted by young Joe Kennedy.* They were in the process of checking out along the way and, for some unknown reason, in the check-out they detonated the explosive, and that was the end of that.

Q: The whole thing blew up in the air.

Captain Barnaby: They never even found enough parts to identify and bury him. And that was what happened to the oldest Kennedy boy--Jack's older brother. They did go on with the project--it didn't die with that--and they were used in the Pacific against some Japanese bases.

Q: They never used them against the submarine pens?

Captain Barnaby: That, I do not know, whether that stopped the project completely or not. I don't know. Someone else could tell. I think Admiral Fahrney would undoubtedly know. By the way, Admiral Fahrney also is associated with the Franklin Institute at Philadelphia. But that was another outgrowth. I mentioned earlier that we had done some glider test work down at Patuxent. We built at the aircraft factory, at the direction of the Bureau of Aeronautics, a glider which was for that purpose. It was to carry a payload of 18,000 pounds of TNT. It was grossed fully loaded at 36,000 pounds.

Q: A far cry from your little glider in 1909.

Captain Barnaby: I know. When they were building the glider, I used to get into the shop and watch the progress on it. As it got near completion, each time I'd look at it, I'd go

---

* Lieutenant Joseph P. Kennedy, Jr. The other man in the plane was Lieutenant Wilford Willy, USN. This failed mission was on 12 August 1944. For a detailed account, see Hank Searls, The Lost Prince: Young Joe, the Forgotten Kennedy; the Story of the Oldest Brother (New York: World Publishing Company, 1969).

home and eat more Wheaties. It was a monster. It was 110-foot span and in the light condition in which we first flew it, it weighed 18,000 pounds. Actually we finally flew it fully loaded to 36,000 pounds.

Q: Without mishap?

Captain Barnaby: Without mishap. But it was another project that was too late and never was carried on. And there were technical reasons also. First of all, it became very apparent that while it sounds easy that you can sit and look at a television picture set in the nose looking directly ahead, it'd be a very simple matter to guide it into a target that you could see there. It isn't simple, at all. In fact, it is very difficult, and it gets increasingly difficult. When you start back, say, ten miles away and at 10,000 feet or something like that, you get loose and you swing the plane around until you get the picture and can see what you're looking for, assuming you can see it that far away, it's quite easy, you can keep it pretty well on. But as you get in closer, it seems to be just the reverse. You know, when you're pulling in a fish, the first part is easy, but when it gets in close it starts whipping so fast. It is the same idea in reverse, in that, for a given lateral displacement, the angle is much different. So that it really is not a practical way to guide a missile. So that's one of the outgrowths of the glider program that I thought might be of interest.

Q: An utterly fascinating angle.

Index To

Reminiscences of

Captain Ralph Stanton Barnaby

U.S. Navy (Retired)

Airships
Possible use of gliders to facilitate landing of dirigibles in the 1930s, 22-23

See also Los Angeles, USS (ZR-3)

Army Air Forces, U.S.
Used bombers for towing other planes in World War II, 45-46

Army Air Service, U.S.
Steps in aviation in the early years of the 20th century, 1, 5-6, 10

B-24 Liberator
Used for unsuccessful attempt to attack German missile sites in France in 1944, 47-48

Baldwin, Captain Thomas Scott, USA
Flew the Army's first dirigible in 1905, later helped youngsters interested in aviation, 5-6

Barnaby, Captain Ralph S., USN (Ret.)
Early interest in the Wright brothers in 1908, 1-4; father of, 2-4; designed and built a glider in 1909, 2-5; he and others organized the New York Model Aero Club in 1909, 5; civilian employment after graduation from Columbia University in 1915, 6-13; joined the Navy in 1917, 13; received the first U.S. soaring certificate in 1929, 14-16; launched a glider from the airship Los Angeles (ZR-3) in January 1930, 15-21; used gliders at Pensacola in 1933 as part of naval aviation training, 24-29, 36; as an engineer at the Naval Aircraft Factory in World War II, 30-32, 46-49; involvement in the Soaring Society over the years, 37-40; commanded the Naval Air Modification Unit, Johnsville, Pennsylvania, in World War II, 43-45

Bolster, Lieutenant Calvin M., CC, USN (USNA, 1920)
Provided support when Barnaby launched a glider from the airship Los Angeles (ZR-3) in January 1930, 15-21

Bureau of Aeronautics
As bureau chief in the 1930s, Rear Admiral Ernest J. King approved a glider training course at Pensacola, 25-26, 28; initiated design studies in World War II for military gliders, 30-32; development in World War II of a glider to carry explosives, 48-49

Clark, Colonel Virginius E., USA
Set up Army aviation engineering center in World War I, 5, 10; as airfoil designer, 10-11

Drones
The Naval Aircraft Factory worked on attack drone development during World War II, 46-47; Lieutenant Joseph P. Kennedy, Jr., was killed in August 1944 in an unsuccessful attempt to send a pilotless B-24 to bomb German rocket sites in France, 47-48

Electric Boat Company
Was approached in 1915 in an unsuccessful attempt by the Gallaudet Engineering Company to gain financing, 7-9

Elmira, New York
Site of soaring meets over the years, 37-41

Fahrney, Captain Delmar S., USN (USNA, 1920)
Worked on the development of attack drones during World War II, 46-48

Figley, Major Richard E., USMC
Experienced an engine failure while serving as a test pilot for the Naval Aircraft Factory in World War II, 43-44

Flight Training
In 1933 the Pensacola Naval Air Station ran prospective students through a glider training course to determine aptitude for flight training, 24-29, 36

Gallaudet Engineering Company
Produced seaplanes for the Navy in the World War I era, 7-9

Germany
Gliding work by Otto Lilienthal in the 1890s, 3; use of zeppelins in World War I, 10; German gliding schools in the 1920s, 14; use of gliders for training in the 1930s and wartime invasion in the 1940s; Wolfgang Klemperer involved in soaring meets in the 1930s, 39

Gliders
Barnaby designed and built his first glider in 1909, 2-5; German gliding schools in the 1920s, 14; Barnaby received the first U.S. soaring certificate in 1929, 14-16; Barnaby launched a glider from the airship Los Angeles (ZR-3) in January 1930, 15-21; possible use of to facilitate landing of dirigibles in the 1930s, 22-23; landing practices during World War II, 23; introduced by the head of the naval test pilot school at Patuxent River, Maryland, in the late 1960s, 24, 36-37, 40; use of at Pensacola in 1933 as part of naval aviation training, 24-29, 36; German use for training in the 1930s and wartime invasion in the 1940s; in World War II, the Naval Aircraft Factory, Philadelphia, did design studies on military gliders, 30-32; use of at Normandy during the invasion of June 1944, 33-34; concept of amphibious gliders, 35, 43; Elmira, New York, has been the site of soaring meets over the years, 37-41; soaring techniques, 41-42; development in World War II of a glider to carry explosives, 48-49

Hughes, Rear Admiral Charles F., USN (USNA, 1888)
As commandant of the Philadelphia Navy Yard around 1920, was prejudiced against aviation, 32-33

Kennedy, Lieutenant Joseph P., Jr, USNR
Killed in August 1944 in a B-24 while trying to make a bombing attack on German rocket sites in France, 47-48

King, Rear Admiral Ernest J., USN (USNA, 1901)
As chief of the Bureau of Aeronautics in the 1930s, approved a glider training course at Pensacola, 25, 28

Lakehurst (New Jersey) Naval Air Station
Site of operation when Barnaby launched a glider from the airship Los Angeles (ZR-3) in January 1930, 15-21

Los Angeles, USS (ZR-3)
Airship from which Barnaby launched a glider over Lakehurst, New Jersey, in January 1930s, 15-21

Mitscher, Commander Marc A., USN (USNA, 1910)
In the 1930s objected to the use of gliders for pilot training at Pensacola, 25

Moffett, Rear Admiral William A., USN (USNA, 1890)
As Chief of the Bureau of Aeronautics in the 1920s-30s, believed in the value of publicity, 13-14; arranged for Barnaby to launch a glider from the airship Los Angeles (ZR-3) in January 1930, 15, 18, 21; contemplated use of gliders in the 1930s to facilitate the landing of airships, 22-23

Naval Aircraft Factory, Philadelphia
Did design studies in World War II on military gliders, 30-32; worked on attack drone development during World War II, 46-47; development in World War II of a glider to carry explosives, 48-49

Naval Air Modification Unit, Johnsville, Pennsylvania
Developed a technique in World War II for towing airplanes with dead engines, 43-45

Normandy, France
Use of gliders during the Allied invasion in June 1944, 33-34

Patuxent River (Maryland) Naval Air Station
Captain Reuben P. Prichard introduced gliders while head of the naval test pilot school in the late 1960s, 24, 36-37, 40

Pensacola Naval Air Station
  Use of gliders in 1933 as preparation for Navy flight training, 24-29, 36

Prichard, Captain Reuben P., Jr., USN (USNA, 1948)
  Introduced gliders while head of the naval test pilot school at Patuxent River, Maryland, in the late 1960s, 24, 36-37, 40

Roché, Jean
  Joined a model airplane club in 1909, later involved with Army aviation and the Aeronca Company, 5, 9-10

SB2U Vindicator
  Towed by a PBY after an engine failure during World War II, 43-44

Soaring
  Elmira, New York, has been the site of soaring meets over the years, 37-41; techniques for remaining aloft, 41-42

Standard Aero Corporation
  Construction in 1916-17 of military training planes, 9-13

Television
  Use in World War II as part of a guidance system for a glider to carry explosives, 48-49

Training
  Use of gliders at Pensacola in 1933 as part of the preparation for Navy flight instruction, 24-29, 36

Weather
  Cold weather when the airship Los Angeles (ZR-3) launched a glider in January 1930, 18-21

World War I
  U.S. industrial work during the wartime era, 6-13; use of aircraft by European powers, 10

Wright, Orville and Wilbur
  Aviation feats in the early years of the 20th century, 1-4, 16; Orville Wright signed Barnaby's 1929 soaring certificate, 14-15

Zogbaum, Captain Rufus S., Jr., USN (USNA, 1901)
  Glider training took place in 1933 while he was commandant of the Pensacola Naval Air Station, 26